Introduction

Music Theory Practice - Level 4 is an invaluable resource for those taking a Grade 4 Music Theory Exam at both ABRSM and Trinity College.

The knowledge in this edition is accumulative in that it assumes that you have already completed *Music Theory Practice - Levels 1 - 3,* and it is recommended that you complete these levels before working through this book.

This book contains not only a detailed explanation of each topic, but practice questions complete with answers for you to test your understanding.

As a music teacher of over 35 years of experience, I have never had a student fail a theory exam. Through my own understanding of what works best for students and how some of the alternative material on the market can sometimes be a very tedious method of learning, I have developed this course as a compliment to my video series on the YouTube channel *MusicOnline UK* and I am confident that you will find success in your exam by going through this course.

PAST PAPER MARKING SERVICE

In addition to the exercises in this book you can make use of the Past Paper Marking Service - FREE to Patrons of MusicOnline UK, so that you can really understand how well you have mastered the various topics. More details available on www.patreon.com/musiconlineuk

So are you ready to get started on your road to Music Theory understanding.....

Lesson 4.1 - Time Signatures - REVIEW

By Grade 4 Music Theory, you need to know all simple and compound time signatures.

To summarize:

For Simple Time Signatures
- Top number tells you how many beats in a bar
- Bottom number tells you the type of beat
  /2 minim beat
  /4 crotchet beat
  /8 quaver beat
  /16 semiquaver beat

Therefore some of the new time signatures you might come across at this level might be
  2/8 - 2 quaver beats in a bar
  4/2 - 4 minim beats in a bar

For Compound Time Signatures

Remember that the beats are grouped into into threes
So for example,
6/4 time, although it contains 6 crotchets in every bar is actually 2 DOTTED MINIM BEATS IN A BAR and the way the notes are grouped will reflect this.
Take a look at this example

The dashes / indicate where the beats are

You will notice that both lines have exactly the same lengths of notes, but in 6/4 time the beats are dotted minims. In 3/2 time, the beats are just minims. The notes need to be grouped together to reflect this.

For example the minim in the first bar needs to be split into two tied crotchets, in 3/2 time, because the two halves belong to different beats.

Similarly, the semibreve at the end must be split into a crotchet tied to a dotted minim in 6/4 time because these two notes belong to two separate beats.

Questions

1. Add a time signature to each of the following bars.

2. Under each bar above, describe the time signature as "simple or compound" **and** as "duple, triple or quadruple.

3. Rewrite the following passage in 3/2 time grouping the notes in minims rather than dotted minims.

Lesson 4.2 - Breves and Double Dotting

Breves

The prefix "semi" on a word means half. Therefore a semibreve is half of a breve and the latter is worth 8 crotchets. This is what a breve and its equivalent rest look like:

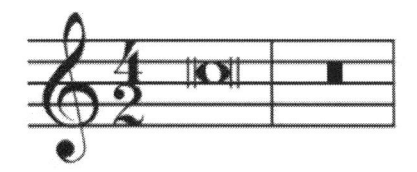

NOTE: Up until now you learned that a whole bar of rest was always indicated by a semibreve rest. However for a whole bar of rest in 4/2 time you would need to put a breve rest as shown above.

Double Dotting

You already should know that dotted notes are worth half as much again as the original note. Double dotting is where there is another "half of the half" added on.

For example:

Minim = 2 crotchets

Dotted minim = 2 plus half of 2 = 3 crotchets

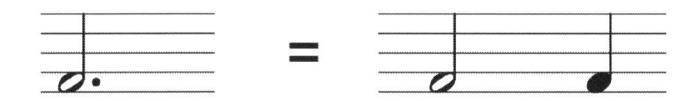

A ***double dotted minim*** =
2 + half of 2 + half of half of 2 = 3 and a half crotchets.

Similarly a double dotted crotchet is worth one and three quarter crotchets and a double dotted quaver is worth seven eighths of a crotchet.

Questions

1. A breve is worth how many
    a) minims
    b) quavers
    c) demisemiquavers?

2. Write the correct rest in each of the places below, marked with an asterisk.

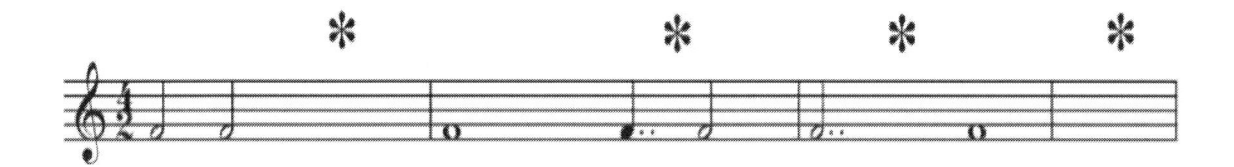

Lesson 4.3 - Duplets

You should already know that triplets are 3 notes played in the space of 2. Duplets are simply 2 notes played in the space of 3 and are shown by placing a bracketed two above the relevant notes.

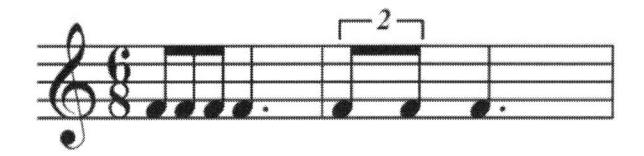

This would be quite useful if you needed to convert a piece from simple time into compound time.

For example, if you were asked to convert this 4/4 rhythm into compound time

it would become

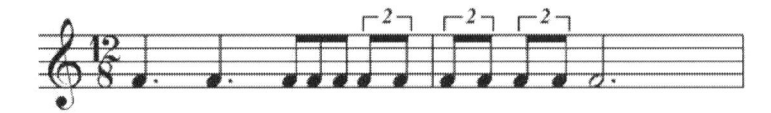

The duplets in this example occur where two notes are played in the space of where you would normally find three.

Remember in 12/8 time a beat normally contains 3 quavers. If you only have 2 notes in a beat - a duplet sign is needed.

Notice also that the crotchet beats of 4/4, become **dotted crotchet beats** in 12/8

Finally note there is no need for the triplet sign used in the 4/4 rhythm because the beat in 12/8 contains 3 quavers anyway.

Questions

1. Write this 3/4 rhythm in 9/8 time so that it sounds the same. The first note has been done for you.

2. Now write this 9/8 rhythm in 3/4 time, again, so that it sounds the same.

3. Now complete this sentence by inserting the words *"duplets", "triplets", "dots"*.

"When converting from simple time to compound time we add _____ and _____ and lose _____ "

4. Now write a similar sentence starting, "When converting from compound time to...............

Lesson 4.4 - Alto Clef

The alto clef is between the treble and bass clef and its middle line is middle C. This is what an alto clef and a Middle C written on it, look like

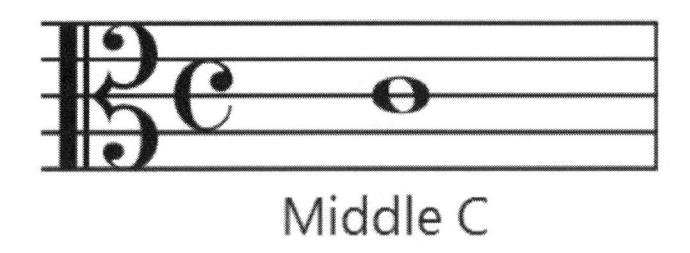

Middle C

Apart from simply naming the notes of the alto clef, an examination may require you to write out a simple melody from treble or bass clef into alto clef or vice versa.

For example - if you had to write this out in treble clef :

it would become this:

You need to be careful that you don't just write the correct letter, but also at the correct octave. Remember that middle C in the alto clef is on the *middle line.*

Questions

1. Name the following notes

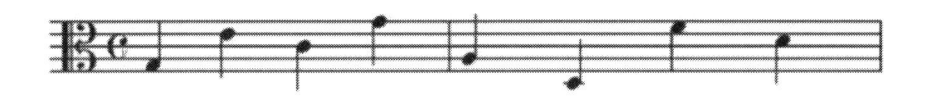

2. Rewrite the following passage into alto clef, using the empty stave below

3. Rewrite the following passage into treble clef, using the empty stave below

Lesson 4.5 - Double Sharps and Double Flats

A sharp raises notes by a semitone - a double sharp raises notes by two semitones. Similarly a double flat lowers notes by two semitones. The symbols used are shown below.

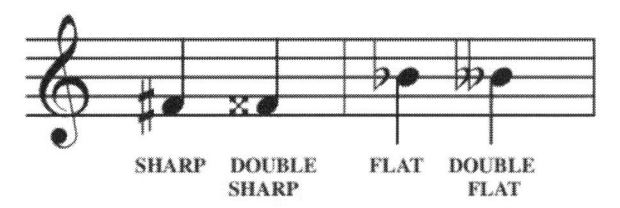

You may have already noticed that all notes have more than one name. For example, F sharp = G flat

Similarly **F double sharp = G** and **G double flat = F**

On the piano keyboard, sometimes there is no black note between two white notes and in this case extra care must be taken. So for example, a B double sharp is the same as a C sharp or D flat.

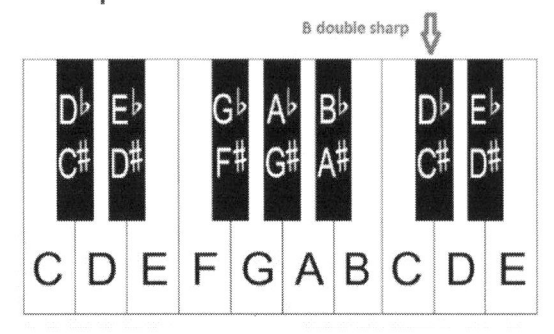

These are called "*enharmonic equivalents*". In fact every note always has two enharmonic equivalents. All the following are in fact the same pitch.

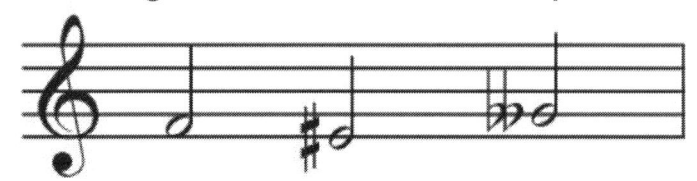

Questions

1. Complete this sentence: "**G double sharp, is an enharmonic equivalent of _____ and _____** .

2. Next two each of these notes, write two more notes that are enharmonic equivalents.

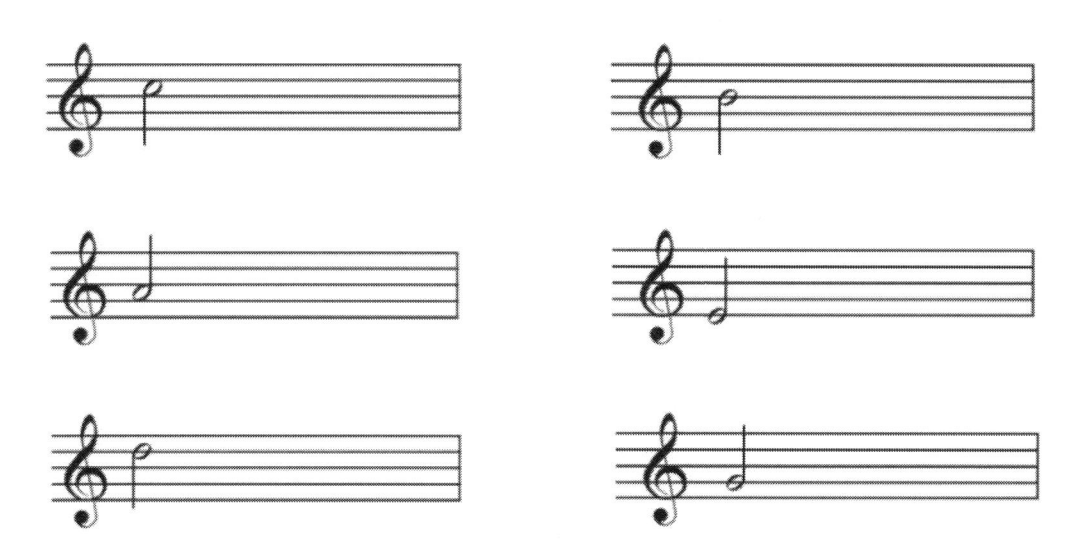

Lesson 4.6 - Keys up to 5 sharps or flats

Major Keys

In level 3 you learned up to 4 sharps or flats, so in this level, there is not that much more to learn. The new scales for this grade are shown in bold in this table.

Key	Key Signature
B major	**F♯, C♯, G♯, D♯, A♯**
E major	F♯, C♯, G♯, D♯
A major	F♯, C♯, G♯
D major	F♯, C♯
G major	F♯
C major	No sharps or flats
F major	B♭
B♭ major	B♭, E♭
E♭ major	B♭, E♭, A♭
A♭ major	B♭, E♭, A♭, D♭
D♭ major	**B♭, E♭, A♭, D♭, G♭**

As was explained in the previous level, there is a pattern of fifths between all these key signatures. Starting at the bottom with D flat major the fifth note of each scale is the scale above in the table. A flat is the fifth note of D flat major, E flat is the fifth note of A flat major etc.

Also the distance between all the sharps and flats is a fifth.
From G flat to D flat is a 5th
From D flat to A flat is a 5th

The same is true with the sharps
From F sharp to C sharp is a 5th
From C sharp to G sharp is a 5th

Here is how these key signatures look in the bass and treble clef

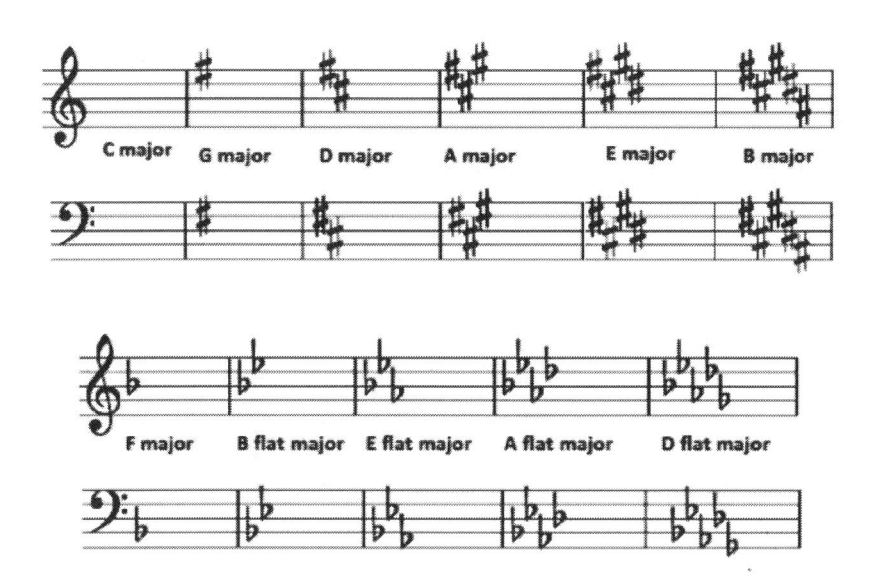

Notice also the pattern of the placement, where you put the sharps or flats. There is a pattern with the sharps that goes high, low, high, low, but the final A sharp breaks the pattern. With the flats it is easier, start low and then alternate high, low, high, low.

Minor Keys
You previously learned that every major key has a relative minor. Therefore the two new major keys you just learned will have two new relative minors. i.e.

G♯ minor is the relative minor of B major ...and
B♭ minor is the relative minor of D♭ major.

But there's more!!

Up until now in this course you have only needed to know the harmonic form of the minor scale with its raised 7th. In Grade 4 ABRSM and Grade 3 Trinity College Music Theory, you also need to know the melodic minor scale.

In a melodic minor scale the 6th and 7th notes are raised on the way up **ONLY** and these notes revert back to the key signature on the way down.

Consider this scale of G minor

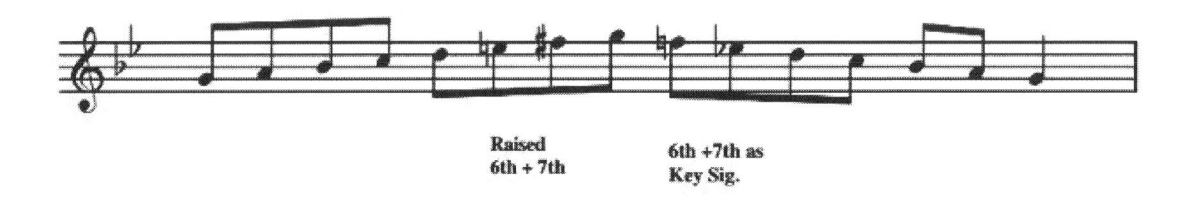

On the way up the 6th and 7th notes which are normally E flat and F, (according to the Key Signature), are raised to E natural and F sharp and on the way down they revert back to F and E flat (as per Key Signature).

This table summarizes all the key signatures of the minor scales you need for this level along with the notes that need to be raised for both harmonic and melodic minor scales.

Key	Key Signature	Harmonic Raise 7th	Melodic Raise 6th & 7th Ascending only
G♯ minor	F♯, C♯, G♯, D♯, A♯	Fx	E♯ & Fx
C♯ minor	F♯, C♯, G♯, D♯	B♯	A♯ & B♯
F♯ minor	F♯, C♯, G♯	E♯	D♯ & E♯
B minor	F♯, C♯	A♯	G♯ & A♯
E minor	F♯	D♯	C♯ & D♯
A minor	No sharps or flats	G♯	F♯ & G♯
D minor	B♭	C♯	B♮ & C♯
G minor	B♭, E♭	F♯	E♮ & F♯
C minor	B♭, E♭, A♭	B♮	A♮ & B♮
F minor	B♭, E♭, A♭, D♭	E♮	D♮ & E♮
B♭ minor	B♭, E♭, A♭, D♭, G♭	A♮	G♮ & A♮

Notice the F double sharp in G♯ minor as you raise the 7th - F♯ to Fx

Questions

1. Name the major key that corresponds to the following key signatures.

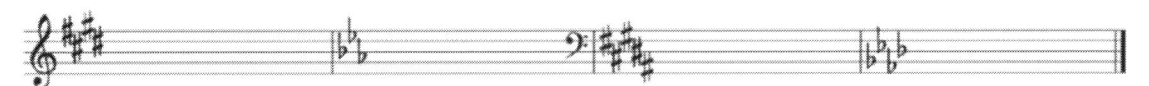

2. Write a key signature of D flat major, taking care of the order and placement of the accidentals.

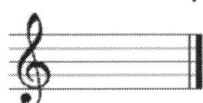

3. Write the following scales **with key signatures** remembering to add **any extra accidentals** that are **not in the key signature.**

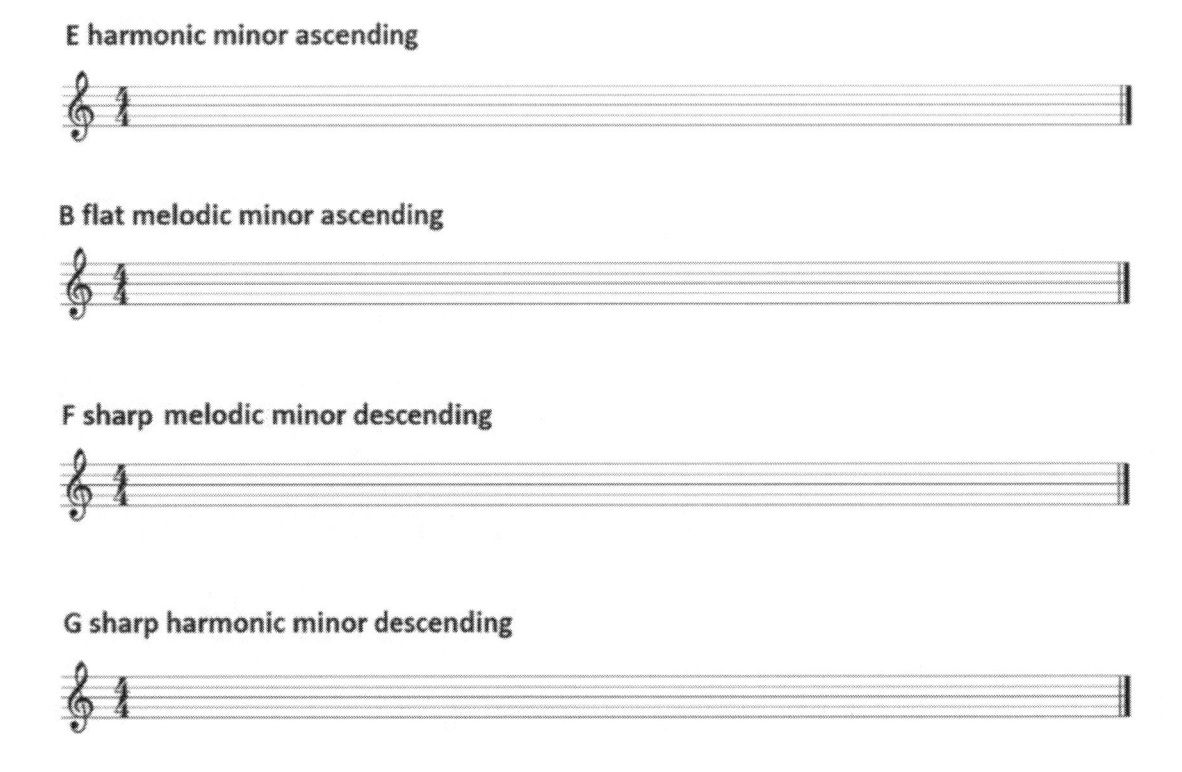

E harmonic minor ascending

B flat melodic minor ascending

F sharp melodic minor descending

G sharp harmonic minor descending

Lesson 4.7 - Technical Names for Degrees of the Scale

This requirement is simply a question of learning seven words corresponding to the seven degrees of the scale - and **you already know the first one!**

In Trinity College Theory they are introduced one or two at a time from Grades 1-6 whereas in ABRSM Music Theory, they are all introduced together at Grade 4.

1st degree of the scale = tonic
2nd degree of the scale = supertonic
3rd degree of the scale = mediant
4th degree of the scale = subdominant
5th degree of the scale = dominant
6th degree of the scale = submediant
7th degree of the scale = leading note
8th degree of the scale = tonic (same as 1st)

There is a pattern to observe that might help you remember some of these. The prefix "sub" means below. So if the dominant is the 5th note *up* from the tonic, then the **sub**dominant is the 5th note *down* from the tonic. The same is true for mediant (3rd note up) and submediant (3rd note down)

... and that's about it. Take a moment to try to memorise these seven terms and then try the questions on the next page.

Questions

1. Given that the first note in each of the bars below is the *key note*, state the technical name for the second note in each bar.

2. In the key of D flat major, write the following notes

Tonic   Submediant   Supertonic

Lesson 4.8 - Writing Chromatic Scales

A chromatic scale is one where every semitone between two given notes is played. When writing a chromatic scale it will mean that you will have to use some letters more than once e.g. a G followed by a G sharp. Generally try to avoid using a particular letter more than twice. i.e. don't write G flat, G, G sharp.

When writing a chromatic scale there will be more than one possible correct answer.

the example shown here could also be written like this

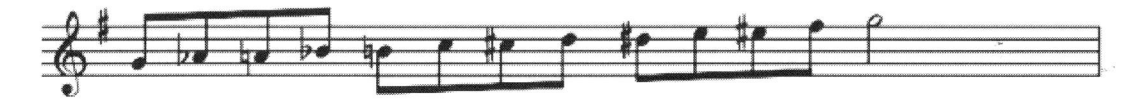

Both these are exactly the same notes, written in two different ways. Notice also the F sharp key signature. You may have to do an exercise with or without a key signature in an examination.

Questions

1. Turn the following into chromatic scales by adding accidentals.

……… *Mind the key signatures here*

2. Write a chromatic scale, starting on the given note, one octave ascending.

NOTE - there is more than one possible correct answer to this question.

Lesson 4.9 - Intervals (Augmented and Diminished)

In level 3, you learned the prefixes major, minor and perfect as applied to intervals. To summarize; 4ths, 5ths and octaves are perfect. 2nds, 3rds, 6ths and 7ths are major if they occur in the major scale of the lower note.

Major 2nd   Major 3rd   Perfect 4th   Perfect 5th   Major 6th   Major 7th   Perfect Octave

Minor intervals are a semitone less than major intervals.

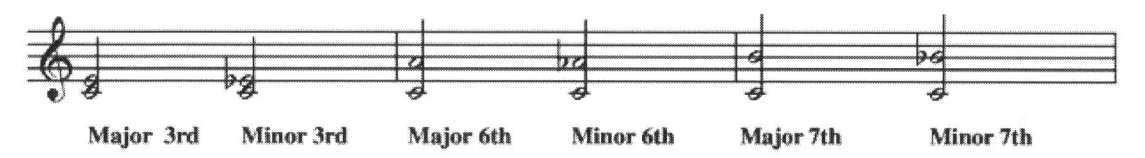

Major 3rd   Minor 3rd   Major 6th   Minor 6th   Major 7th   Minor 7th

In this lesson there are two *more* prefixes as applied to intervals: **Augmented and Diminished.**

- Perfect and major intervals can be augmented (increased by a semitone)

- Perfect and minor intervals can be diminished (decreased by a semitone).

Let's consider some examples

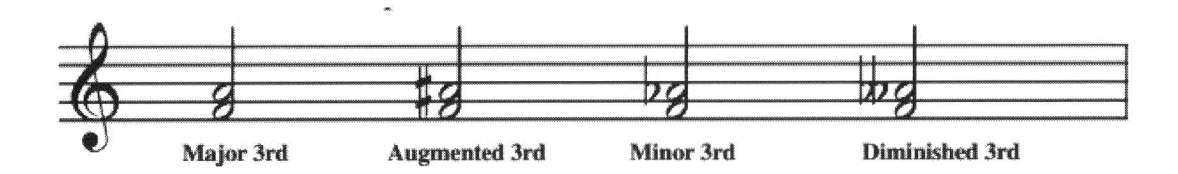

Major 3rd *Augmented 3rd* *Minor 3rd* *Diminished 3rd*

- F to A is a ***major*** 3rd (A is the 3rd note of F major)
- F to A sharp is an ***augmented*** 3rd (increased by a semitone)
- F to A flat is a ***minor*** 3rd (decreased by a semitone)
- F to A double flat is a ***diminished*** 3rd (a minor 3rd decreased by yet another semitone).

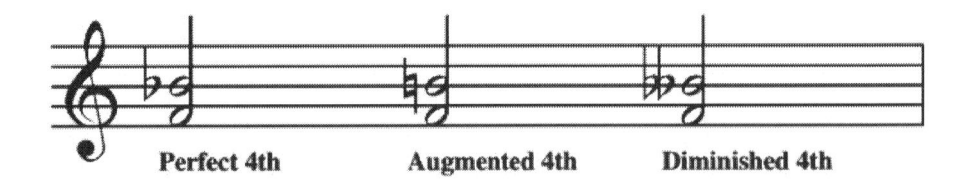

Perfect 4th *Augmented 4th* *Diminished 4th*

- F to B flat is a ***perfect*** 4th (B flat is the 4th note of F major and remember there is no such thing as a major or minor 4th)
- F to B natural is an ***augmented*** 4th. (Increased by a semitone).
- F to B double flat is a ***diminished*** 4th (Decreased by a semitone).

Many people find this quite complicated but if you follow this flow chart you can't go wrong.

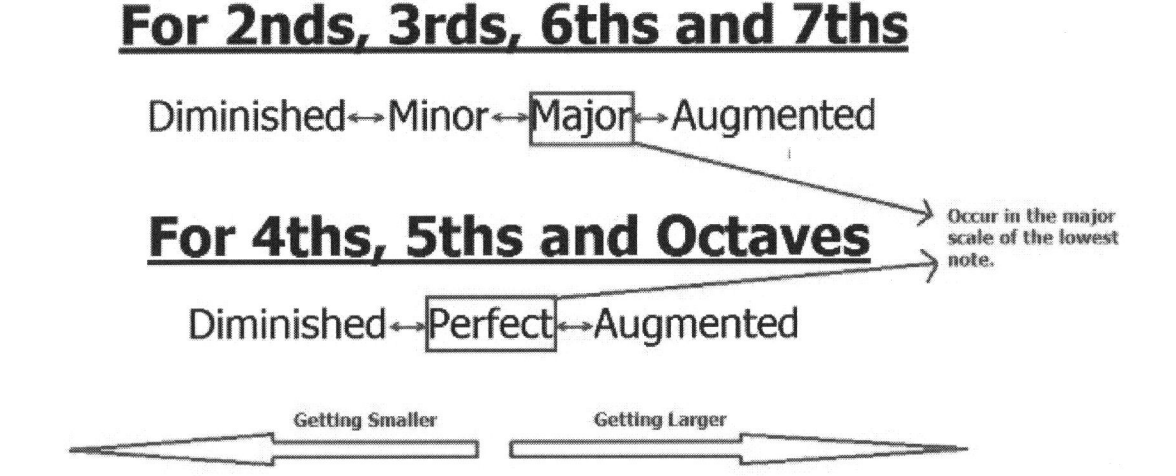

For 2nds, 3rds, 6ths and 7ths

Diminished ↔ Minor ↔ Major ↔ Augmented

For 4ths, 5ths and Octaves

Diminished ↔ Perfect ↔ Augmented

Occur in the major scale of the lowest note.

← Getting Smaller   Getting Larger →

For 2nds, 3rds, 6ths & 7ths

- If the upper note is in the major scale of the lower note it is MAJOR
- If it is a semitone less it is MINOR
- If it is a semitone more it is AUGMENTED
- If it is 2 semitones less it is DIMINSHED

For 4ths, 5ths and Octaves.

- If the upper note is in the major scale of the lower note it is PERFECT.
- If it is a semitone less it is DIMINSHED
- If it is a semitone more it is AUGMENTED.

The only problem may arise if the lower note is one you do not know the major scale of, C sharp to A flat for example.

If you asked the interval between C sharp and A flat first consider the major scale of a note you do know i.e. C major.

Now C - A is a major 6th

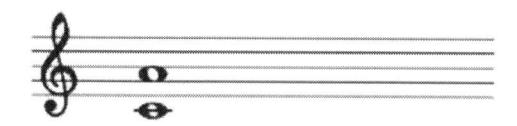

A is the 6th note of C major
So C - A is a major 6th

...so C# to A is a semitone less i.e. a minor 6th

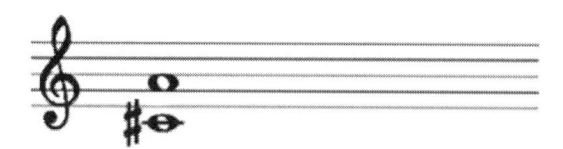

C sharp - A is one semitone smaller than C - A so this is a minor 6th

and C# to Ab would be a diminished 6th

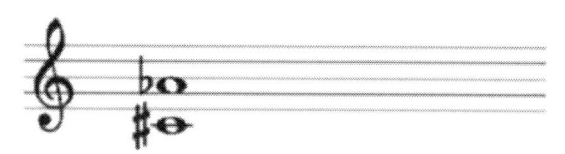

A flat is yet another semitone closer to C sharp than A, so this interval is a diminished 6th

Questions

Name the interval between the two notes in each bar

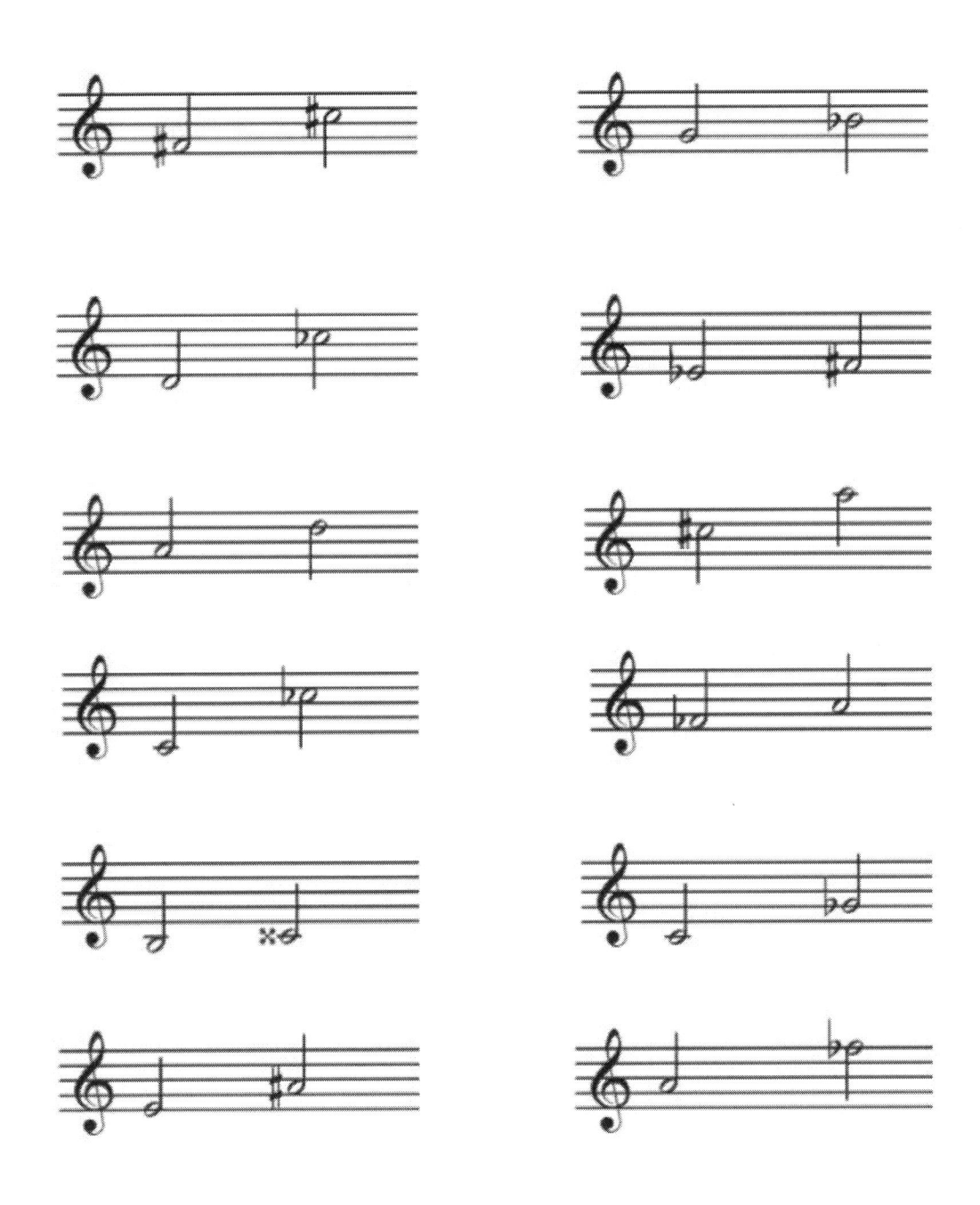

Lesson 4.10 - Writing and Recognizing Chords

The chords you will need to know for Grade 4 ABRSM Music Theory, are those built on the Tonic, the Subdominant and the Dominant. You will remember these are the 1st, 4th and 5th degrees of the scale.

Trinity College introduces the Dominant chord in Grade 3 and the Subdominant in Grade 4.

Previously you have come across the Tonic Triad where a chord was built on the key note - the "tonic" using the 1st, 3rd and 5th degrees of the scale. The principle is the same for the two new chords, but you just need to build the chord starting on the 4th or 5th degree of the scale. Here are the three triads in the key of E major.

Tonic Triad

Subdominant Triad

Dominant Triad

There are two other things to bear in mind in this topic:

1. In a minor key the dominant triad contains the 7th degree of the scale and you will remember that the 7th note of a harmonic minor is raised. So for example in the scale of E *minor* - the 7th note is raised to D sharp. This 7th degree of the scale occurs in the dominant triad and so the dominant triad contains a D sharp. In fact the middle note of the dominant triad in any minor key is raised.

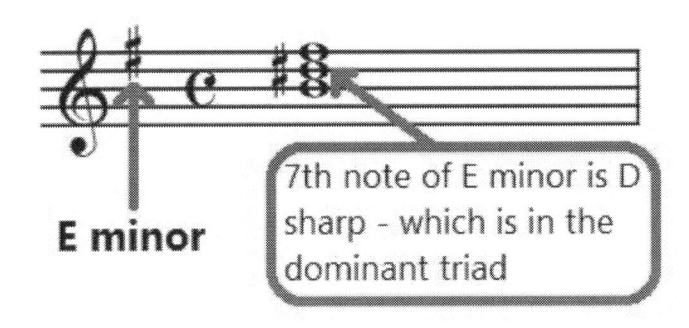

E minor

7th note of E minor is D sharp - which is in the dominant triad

2. Triads may be written in "open position" which means that all the notes might not necessarily be close to each other. They may even cover two clefs. The trick to easily recognizing the chord, is to look at the bass note. Both the chords here, for example are a tonic triad of C major.

Tonic C major   Tonic C major

Questions

1. Name these chords in "*open position*".
The Key is D flat major

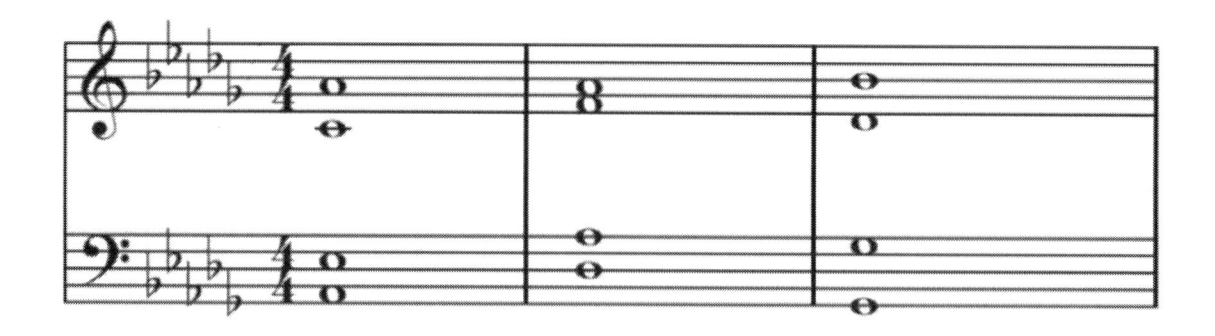

2. Write the chords asked for in *"closed position"*.
The Key is F sharp minor.

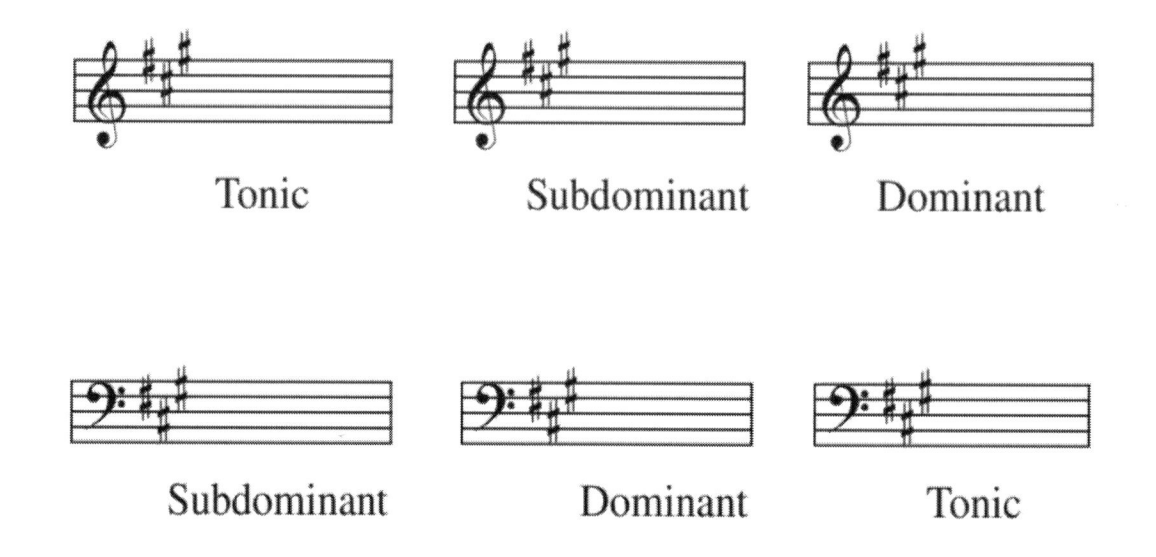

Tonic   Subdominant   Dominant

Subdominant   Dominant   Tonic

Lesson 4.11 - Ornaments

There are 6 types of ornament you need to know for Grade 4 ABRSM / Grade 5 Trinity Music Theory.

An ornament is a note or group of notes that "decorate" the main melody note. You will only need to know the names of the signs at this stage and will **NOT** be required to write out how the ornament sounds.

Trill

A trill is a rapid alternation between the written note and the note above it. Sometimes there may be a small turn at the end, don't let this put you off. Also depending on the period of music the starting note may be the written note *or* the upper note.

Turn

There are two kinds of turn you need to know. The first is the turn **on** a note where you start on the upper note, then a rapid triplet descending down through the main note to the lower note and returning to the main note.

The second type is a turn *between* notes. In this case you start with the written note, before doing the rapid triplet as above

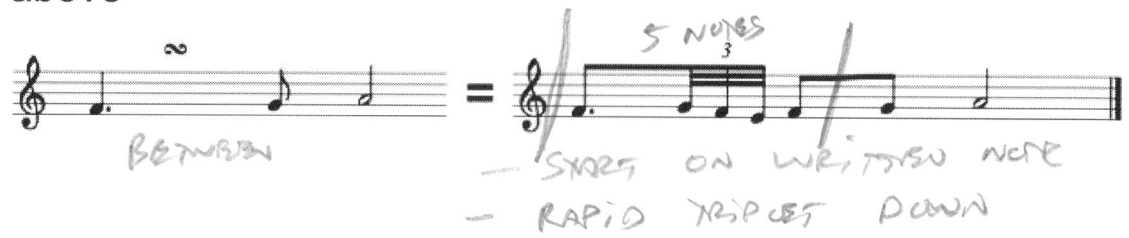

(5 NOTES)

BETWEEN
- START ON WRITTEN NOTE
- RAPID TRIPLET DOWN

Mordents

Again there are two types, the upper and lower mordent, they both start on the main written note and rapidly move one step away and back again, the only difference between the two being, the upper mordent steps up and the lower mordent steps down. Notice the slash in the sign for a lower mordent.

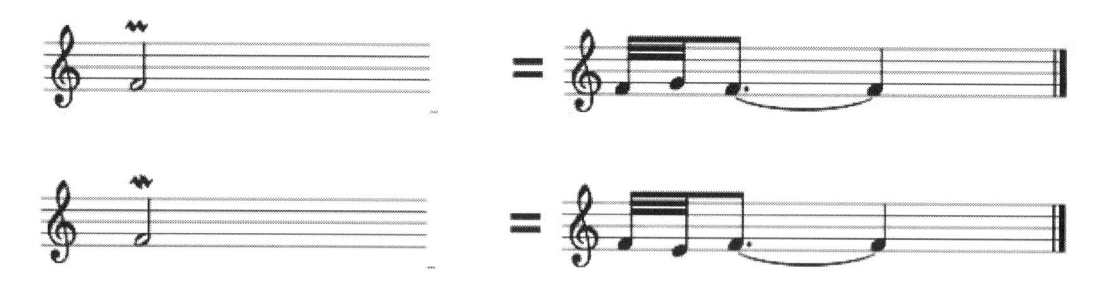

Acciaccatura

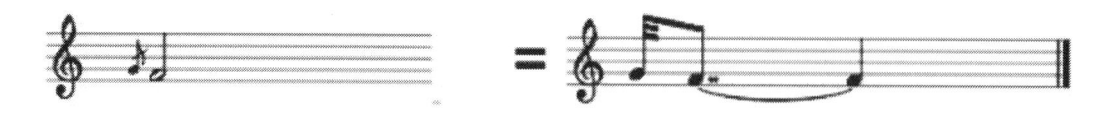

This is often called a **grace note** and may be called such in an exam. It is also sometimes referred to as a crush note describing its effect of rapidly crushing the smaller note just before and onto the main written note. However, this term is best avoided in the exam, even if it is helpful in remembering its function.

Appoggiatura

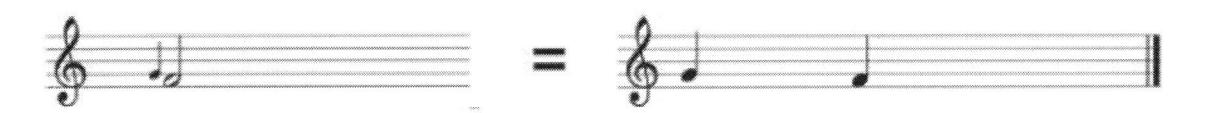

The effect of an Appoggiatura is very similar to that of the acciaccatura, except is is slower, often dividing the time value of the main written note in half. Notice the sign for the appoggiatura, does *not* have the "slash" through it like the grace note.

Questions

1. Name the following ornaments.

2. Name the following ornaments written out in full.

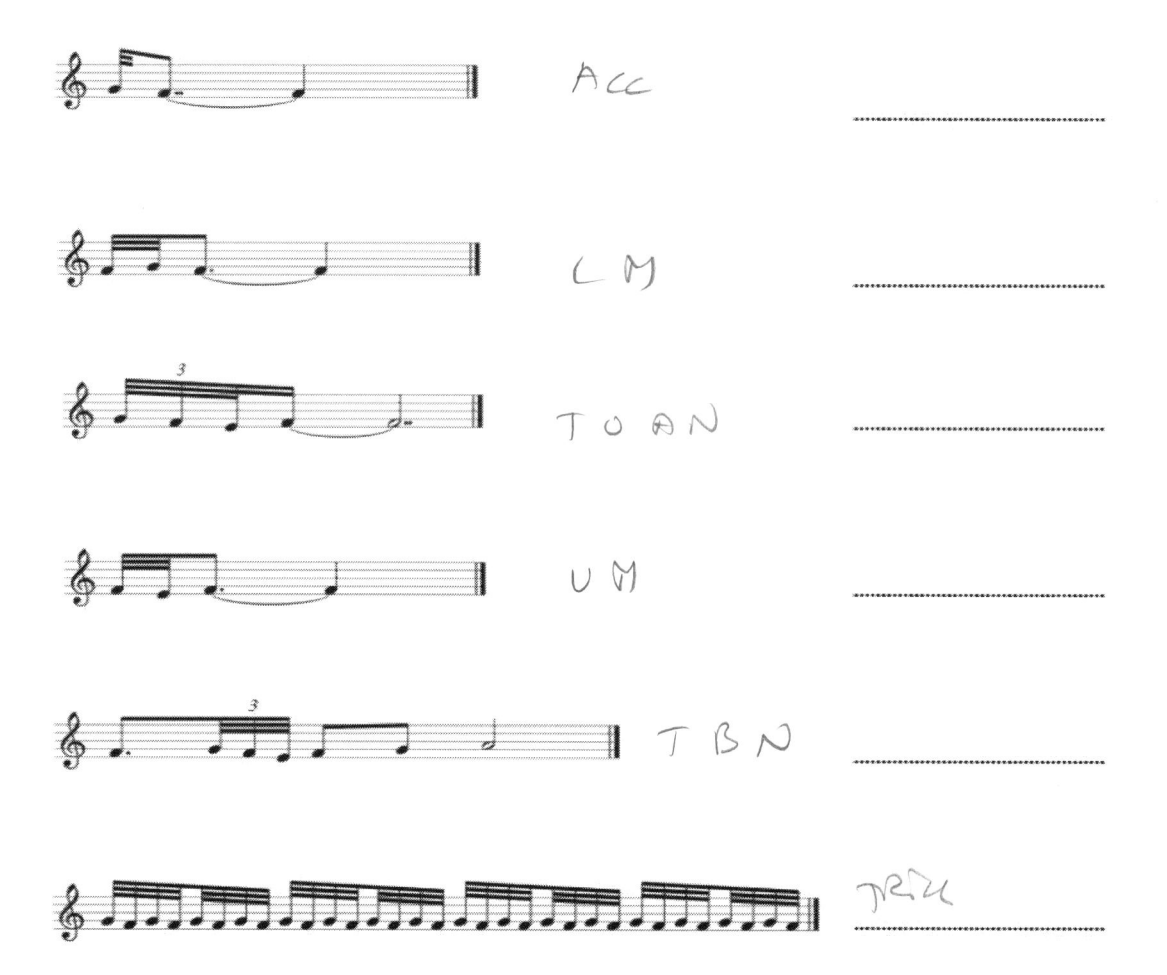

Acc

LM

TUAN

UM

TBN

TR↲

Lesson 4.12 - Orchestral Instruments

Some basic questions about the instruments of the orchestra will be asked at examination for Grade 4 ABRSM Music Theory. In Trinity College Music Theory exams, this knowledge starts at Grade 3 but only for a limited number of instruments, namely violin, cello, flute and bassoon.

Questions might include:
- the names of the different instruments and to which orchestral family they belong.
- the range of these instruments and a knowledge of which clefs are used by them.
- some terms and signs that apply specifically to certain instruments

Instrument families (arranged in pitch order high-low)
- **Strings:**
Violin, Viola, Cello, Double Bass
- **Woodwind:**
Flute, Oboe, Clarinet, Bassoon
- **Brass:**
Trumpet, Horn, Trombone, Tuba
- **Percussion:**
Timpani, Xylophone, Drums (various kinds) Cymbals etc.

One common questions with regard to percussion instruments is to differentiate between tuned (those that possess a specific pitch or pitches e.g. timpani) and untuned (those that have no specific pitch e.g. bass drum). The above lists are by no means exhaustive but do list some of the more popular instruments

Clefs

The majority of instruments use the treble clef most of the time with the exceptions of the following -

Alto Clef - Viola

Tenor Clef - Tenor Trombone

Bass Clef - Cello, Double Bass, Bassoon, Bass Trombone and Tuba

Other instruments may use other clefs sometimes, but the ones given above are the most commonly used.

Instrument Specific Terms and Signs

Sordini (or sord) - Mutes as used by stringed and brass instruments.

The following signs are used just by string instruments.

1. Down bow
2. Up bow
3. Play the notes within the slur with one bow
4. Short for pizzicato meaning plucked
5. On the G string
6. Play near the bridge

The final set of terms and signs are more specifically for the piano.

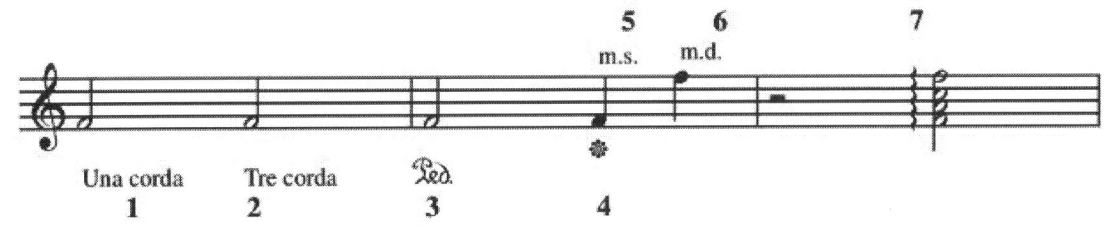

1. Una corda stands for 'one string'* which is to use the left pedal (damper pedal) on the piano

2. Tre corda or 'three strings' means to lift the left (damper) pedal.

3. Ped is short for 'pedal' meaning use the right or sustain pedal.

4. Release the right (sustain) pedal.

5. m.s. - mano sinistra i.e. play with the left hand.

6. m.d. - mano destra i.e. play with the right hand.

7. Spread the notes of a chord, starting at the bottom much like a rapid arpeggio.

*The term Una Corda comes from the fact that traditionally on a piano the sound is made quieter by moving the hammer that hit the strings to one side so that it only strikes one of three strings.

Questions

1. Name a brass instrument that uses the bass clef.

2. What does the abbreviation *pizz.* mean?

3. What instrument is most likely to play the passage below?

4. What clues in the passage led you to your answer for Question 3?

Lesson 4.13 - Musical Terms

Below is a table of terms and signs which are needed for a Grade 4 Theory Exam. Note that in ABRSM you will need to know some **French Terms** as well as Italian ones. To test yourself on these, try our FREE flashcards web app on: https://www.music-online.org.uk/p/lesson-413-theory-quiz-0.html

Italian Terms

affettuoso	tenderly
affrettando	hurrying
amabile	amiable, pleasant
appassionato	with passion
calando	getting softer, dying away
cantando	singing
come	as, similar to
facile	easy
fuoco	fire
giusto	proper, exact
l'istesso	the same
morendo	dying away
niente	nothing
nobilmente	nobly
perdendosi	dying away
possibile	possible
quasi	as if, resembling
sonoro	resonant, with rich tone
sopra	above
sotto	below
veloce	swift
voce	voice

French Terms

à	to, at
animé	animated, lively
assez	enough, sufficient
avec	with
cédez	yield, relax with speed
douce	sweet
en dehors	prominent
et	and
légèrement	light
lent	slow
mais	but
moins	less
modéré	at a moderate speed
non	not
peu	little
plus	more
presser	hurry
ralentir	slow down
retenu	held back
sans	without
très	very
un / une	one
vif	lively
vite	quick

Answers

Lesson 4.1 - Answers

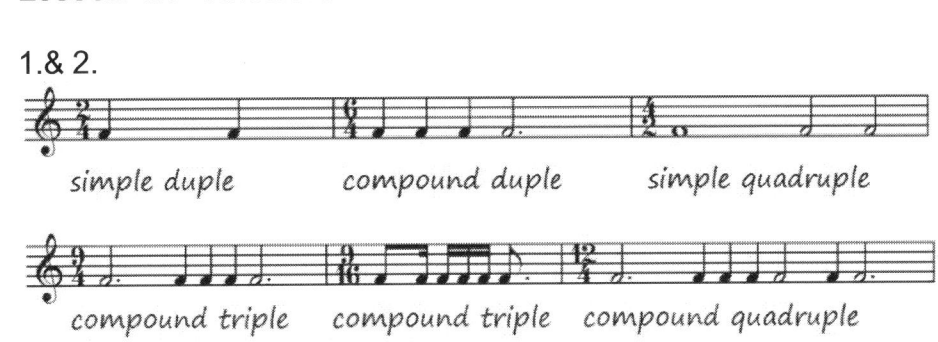

1.& 2.

simple duple   *compound duple*   *simple quadruple*

compound triple   *compound triple*   *compound quadruple*

3.

Lesson 4.2 - Answers

1. a) 4   b) 16   c) 64

2.

Lesson 4.3 - Answers

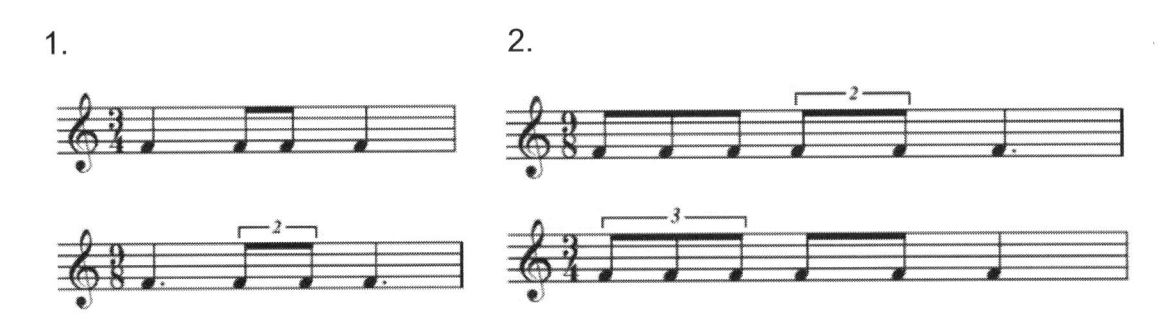

1.

2.

3. When converting from simple time to compound time we add duplets and dots and lose triplets.

4. When converting from compound time to simple time we add triplets and lose duplets and dots.

Lesson 4.4 - Answers

1.

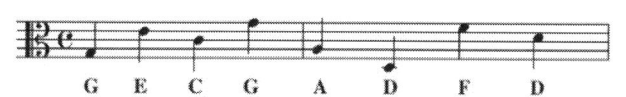

G　E　C　G　A　D　F　D

2.

3.

Lesson 4.5 - Answers

1. "G double sharp, is an enharmonic equivalent of A and B double flat.

2.

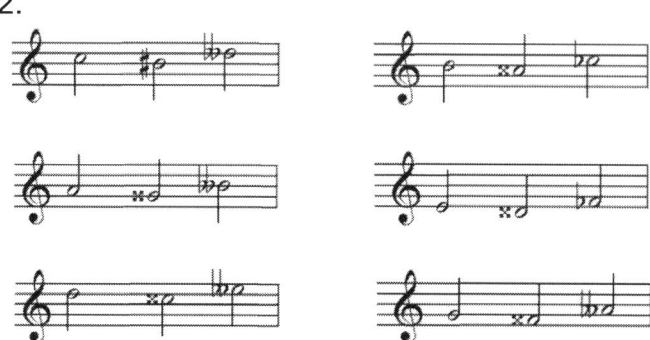

Lesson 4.6 - Answers

1.

E major　　　E flat major　　　B major　　　A flat major

2.

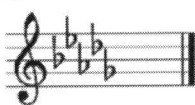

3.

E harmonic minor ascending

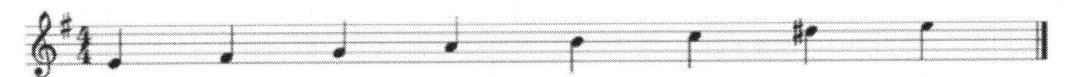

B flat melodic minor ascending

F sharp melodic minor descending

G sharp harmonic minor descending

Lesson 4.7 - Answers

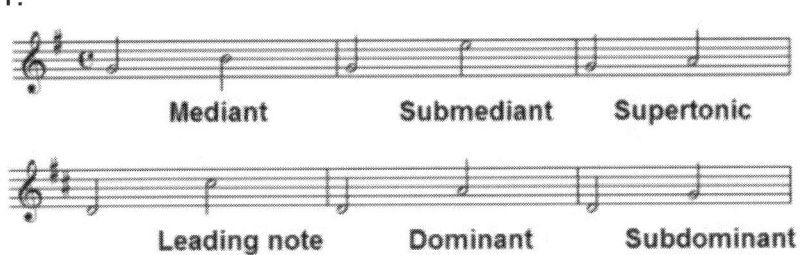

1.

Mediant   Submediant   Supertonic

Leading note   Dominant   Subdominant

2.

Tonic   Submediant   Supertonic

Lesson 4.8 - Answers

1.

2.

N.B. This is only one of various possible answers

Lesson 4.9 - Answers

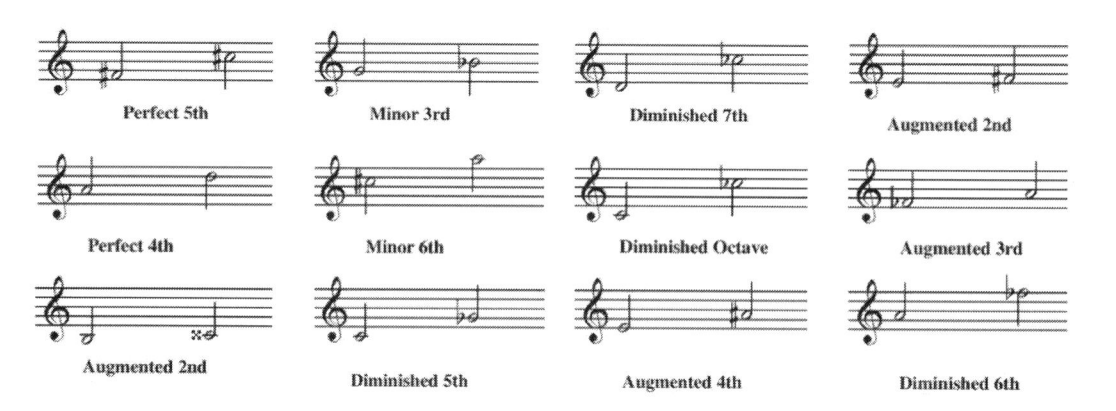

Perfect 5th — Minor 3rd — Diminished 7th — Augmented 2nd

Perfect 4th — Minor 6th — Diminished Octave — Augmented 3rd

Augmented 2nd — Diminished 5th — Augmented 4th — Diminished 6th

Lesson 4.10 - Answers

1.

Dominant — Tonic — Subdominant

2.

Tonic   Subdominant   Dominant

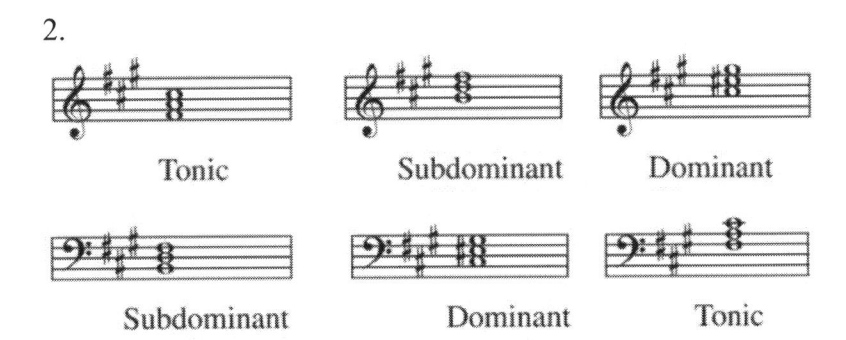

Subdominant   Dominant   Tonic

Lesson 4.11 - Answers

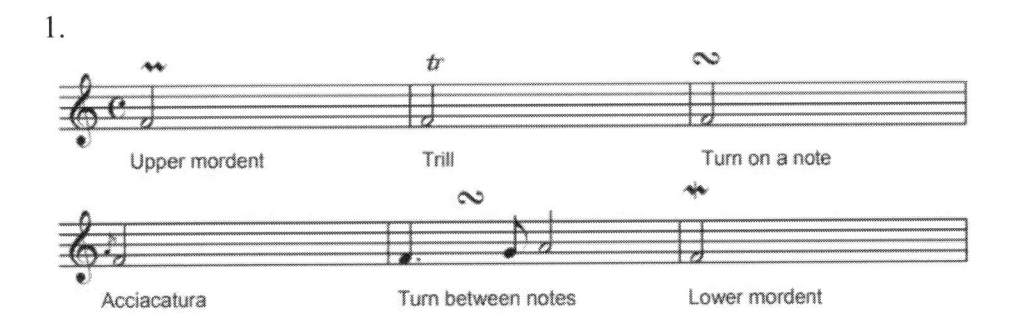

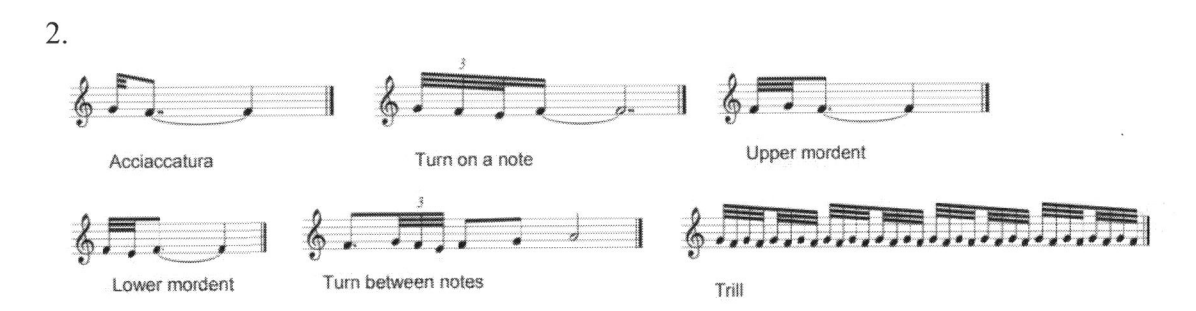

1.

Upper mordent   Trill   Turn on a note

Acciacatura   Turn between notes   Lower mordent

2.

Acciaccatura   Turn on a note   Upper mordent

Lower mordent   Turn between notes   Trill

Lesson 4.12 - Answers

1. Tuba or Trombone

2. Pizzicato - meaning to pluck the string

3. Viola

4. The use of a) the alto clef and b) up bow and down bow markings